From Lemons to **LEMONADE**

Faith-Building Stories From Real Women

Olivia Hudson and Friends

*Thanks for your support.
I hope you enjoy.
Olivia
Jeremiah 29:11-14*

Mary Hopkin

Mother's Day Gift
from my beloved
daughter. Dawn,
May 10, 2015.

From Lemons to Lemonade: Faith building stories from real women
Copyright © 2015 Olivia Hudson

No part of this material may be reproduced, copied, translated, duplicated, mechanically or electronically without the permission of Olivia Hudson.

Printed in the United States of America.

All scriptures quotations, unless indicated are taken from the New International Version
Scriptures taken from the Holy Bible, New International Version®, NIV®.Copyright © 1973, 1978, 1984, 2011 by Biblica, Inc.™ Used by permission of Zondervan. All rights reserved.

The Living Bible copyright © 1971 by Tyndale House Foundation. Used by permission of Tyndale House Publishers Inc., Carol Stream, Illinois 60188. All rights reserved.

Scripture taken from *The Message*. Copyright © 1993, 1994, 1995, 1996, 2000, 2001, 2002. Used by permission of NavPress Publishing Group.

Front Photo by Angela Moreno
Cover Design by Rob Williams - fiverr.com/cal5086
Interior Design by Cory Sr and Olivia Hudson

http://fantasticfivemama.weebly.com

Foreword

I am honored to write the foreword for this book. But when I really think about it, if anyone should write this, it should be me. Why? Because I've not only witnessed the amount of heart and effort that has gone into its creation; but I've reaped the most benefits from the growth and maturing that has occurred during its development.

Years ago, Olivia had dreamed of writing a book that could help Christian military spouses; because after she decided to become a Christian, it was very challenging for her. Unfortunately, someone whose opinion she valued at that time, unknowingly, derailed her dream. Although my wife was discouraged, she never let up on her convictions to help others see that walking with God is the answer to any situation.

One of the benefits of moving around so much for my military assignments is the amount of friends and relationships that have developed over the years. These are more than the random "friends" in social media; these are people who can be called upon to talk to and stay connected with; also they can be called upon when help is needed, just as they were called for the development of the book that you are now holding.

This book contains in its pages women from all walks of life. When you take the time to go along with them and share their life experiences, you'll discover that maybe...just maybe...what you are going through right now is shaping you for something to come, or maybe the discovery of new strength that you did not know you were capable of.

The closer this book came to completion, the closer I saw my wife come to life as one of her dreams of publishing a book to help others was actually happening. It was not an easy process, but she embraced it. Embraced with uncertainty, the range of the emotions that were revisited as she delved into her past to gather the ingredients for what would ultimately become refreshment for others to benefit from.

Since I helped with some of the editing, I was reminded that the ingredients of life include the good and the bad; however at the end of every struggle or challenge, no matter how big or small, we will learn and can share with others so that they can ignite the unexpected flavors that are sometimes hidden in the unfortunate events in our lives.

This book may be the sweetener you've needed to open up your own lemonade stand.

Cory Hudson Sr.

ACKNOWLEDGMENTS

I want to thank God for giving me exactly who I needed when I needed them to make this possible. I have so many people to thank for their contributions to this book!

My beloved husband and children who have supported me in words and actions through the making of this book since the day the idea was born.

My friends Angela Moreno, Alisa Rolle, Mitsuyo Sprague, Tracey V. Page, Candice Fathi and Zenja Glass who volunteered hours of their time to help me with editing, illustration and lots of brainstorming ideas.

My parents who support me and love me.

Thank you to all who prayed, laugh and sometimes cried with me. Thank you for walking with me on this adventure!

To God be the Glory!

Contents

Forward..4
Acknowledgements..6
Introduction..8
  1. A New Beginning...13
  2. Between a ROCK and a HARD
       Place!..20
  3. A New Stage of Life......................................25
  4. 911--- What's the Nature of your
      Emergency?...29
  5. A Moment to Remember..............................33
  6. Unexpected Blessings..................................39
  7. A Cinderella Story......................................46
  8. The Promise...52
  9. Out of My Comfort Zone............................56
10. The Great Comforter....................................60
11. Finding Freedom in Forgiveness...................67
12. God Always Has a Plan................................72
13. The Peace Box...79
14. An Unexpected Journey................................82
15. The Gift 87
16. Grass does Not Grow Under My Feet............93
17. My Milagros..97
18. Jasmine Story..105
19. Note from the Author.................................107
20. Your Lemonade Story................................110

Introduction

Since I was little, writing has always been my form of escape from the torments in my life. When I write I feel free, because I don't feel judged, and I don't have to measure my words or think about my grammar. It doesn't matter if I have the right facial expression or even if I make sense. Writing is what has kept me dreaming, kept me hoping and kept me safe.

In 1995 I became a Christian, which was the best decision I ever made in my life. Now, I'm writing to someone, not just to thin air or to myself. I share my thoughts, my fears, my joys, and my disappointments with God. As time passed, I began to share this with my friends. If someone were having a hard time, I would pull out one of the writings from my journal and share it with them.

The more I shared, the more I heard over and over, "you should write a book". I have heard that same statement for twenty years. I often began to write but I never followed through due to fear. I have tons of writings on what I have learned and continue to learn. Some of the topics include:
- How to open your heart even if you have to pry it open.
- How to remember that you are a

- married woman and not a single mom even though your husband is not around as much as you want.
- What to do when your adult children make choices that hurt you.
- How to walk a road that God has clearly marked out for you when all you know is how it starts but not how it ends.
- How to embrace a child that you did not give birth to while she hurts you because she is so hurt.
- How to care for the little girl inside you that you didn't even know was hurting until you turned thirty.

Those are just some of the things I have written about. Even though there are many topics, I never felt that each one individually was good enough for a book, because I have such a long way to go to be considered wise in any of these areas.

One day I said to my beloved husband of 22 years, "honey, you know how much I want to write a book and you know how much I have been encouraged to do so. You know I love how God can use the bad and turn it into good. You know that it is my desire to help women see that God is a God of comfort and of love and that he does not leave us nor forsake us in spite of what we are going through. You, who know me the best, what will you encourage me to write about?"

His response is what inspired me to write this book, "Honey I think you are trying to fit into a box and you are trying to think of what the women that read your book want to hear. However you are not a "fit into a box" type of woman. You are complex and have not just one focus to share but many and you are good at writing about life and how you deal with it, so I know this may sound generic but write about life...your life. You don't have to fit it into a topic and if you do, it won't be you. You think outside the box and that is what makes you. So don't focus on a topic, just write."

After hearing him I told him that my writing should be something simple like making lemonade out of lemons and he said, "Yes!" That is how this book came about.

This book is a collection of how lemonade was made from lemons in my life. It's not just my lemons, but I also asked a few close friends whom over the years, it's been an honor for me to enjoy watching God create the most delicious lemonade. I hope you enjoy my lemonade stand; there are many flavors, but they all have one thing in common: they started with a lemon, which although was the bitter ingredient, it became so sweet when the sugar, water and other flavors were added. I would not have a lemonade stand of life if I didn't have lemons. In this book I celebrate the lemons that produced very delicious sweet, sweet, lemonade.

My prayer for any woman who reads this is that you will embrace the lemons in your life and that one day, after you have persevered, you will enjoy sweet lemonade and give Glory to God. Remembering the words of James 1:12 *"Blessed is the one who perseveres under trial because, having stood the test, that person will receive the crown of life that The Lord has promised to those who love Him."*

The following is a quote from a very close friend named Zenja Glass, who has allowed God to make lemonade from her lemons. Her words represent the heart of every story in this book:

"For those of you going through present trials and tribulations, don't lose heart! Don't you dare lose heart! Don't you dare run away from seeing God's deliverance! Don't you dare give Satan the glory! Don't you dare give up on life! Don't you dare believe the lies Satan is telling you! Don't you dare forget Jeremiah 29:11! Don't you dare give in to depression! Don't you dare believe your life would be better off if you were dead! Don't you dare think God isn't near you! Don't you dare think God doesn't care! He does care!

That is why He is desperately trying to get you to look up and see Him! See His face! See His deliverance! See His plan for your life!"

1
A New Beginning

I left Panamá at the age of seventeen, running from a life of dysfunction and pain in search of a life of love and happiness. I wanted and needed a new beginning; I was excited to start over. However, I learned very quickly that a new place doesn't mean a new beginning.

All my life my dad suffered from mental illness. The lack of resources in Panamá prevented him from managing his mental illness successfully. He unintentionally hurt many people, and although he tried his best, life at home was sometimes extremely difficult due to the lack of guidance my parents had to address my dad's mental illness. My mom tried her best to make things normal but in spite of her efforts my dad's illness produced very little results in creating a safe environment for our household.

My mom, like most moms, wanted what was best for her children. I am sure my dad wanted the same, but sadly he was not able to be the dad he desired to be.

As my siblings and I grew older, my mom made plans to relocate us to the US. She believed that we would have a fresh start and a better chance of breaking our family legacy. One by one, she moved all her children to the US to live with different family members after we graduated from high school.

I flew into Brooklyn, NY in 1990, excited and ready to embrace a new life. I believed the day I stepped foot on the airplane at Tocumen International Airport in Panamá, that I was leaving the pain behind. I didn't only wave goodbye to family and friends, I was convinced I was waving goodbye to the trauma. I was so happy.

Within weeks I quickly learned that starting over was not going to be as easy as I wanted. There I was, in a new place with new people, and given a new beginning, but this new beginning only exposed more of who I had become and was trying to escape. I was insecure, scared, manipulative, dishonest, arrogant, full of worry and unable to trust anyone, including myself.

Leaving Panamá did not mean leaving me. No matter how much I tried, I could not run from myself, so I developed a way for others (and myself) to ignore the real me. I would wear a mask that made me appear perfect. This mask was very powerful and convincing; even I could not tell the real me even if you had pointed her out. I learned to ignore my pain by becoming overly concerned about helping others or staying so busy that I never had time to be alone with myself.

In 1992 I gave birth to my first born and said, "I do" to my husband. I had an amazing husband, a beautiful baby boy and I was safe. Life was good. I had managed to temporarily bury my past during the day. At night however, when it was quiet and my husband and son were sleeping, I found myself crying with no one to comfort me. I knew I was hurting inside but I refused to be vulnerable and get help for the pain that was stealing my internal joy. I was afraid to let others see who I really was. I was afraid to remove my mask. I didn't want to be judged or misunderstood and I also wanted to enjoy the present and all the good things I had in my life. Life was good.

After I had my first son, I began to experience episodes where my body would become weak and I could barely walk. Sometimes I would become so weak that I had to be taken to the emergency room by ambulance. After months of testing and trying to get to the bottom of these episodes, the doctor said I was very healthy and he had no answers for me.

As I had done with everything else, instead of getting a second opinion, I decided to figure out a way to live with it.

Although I was afraid there was something really wrong with me, and after sharing my fears with those who cared about me, I opted to wear my "I am OK" mask instead.

In 1995 I was invited to join a San Diego International Church of Christ worship service. Accepting that invitation took me on a journey that changed the course of my life and continues to do so. Joyful and very warm people greeted me and made me feel like I was at home. The people I came in contact with were not afraid to talk about their struggles, and didn't seem concerned about being judged or someone gossiping about their shortcomings. This puzzled me. I was hungry for friendship so I stuck around and joined any event the church members invited me to.

The more time I spent with my new friends, the more I learned that facing their weaknesses was a way of life. One day they invited me to sit down with a small group of women to have a personal Bible study. It was then I realized their secret to facing struggles. Their secret was found in imitating Jesus daily.

Through personal Bible studies, God opened the eyes of my heart (Psalm 119:18) and I saw wonderful things in His law. I learned new ways to deal with life and to slowly take my mask off and not be afraid to expose the real me.

As I did so, I felt the love and acceptance that only Jesus can teach. I fell in love with all Jesus stood for. He gave me a voice and showed me that I do not have to live by fear. On May 26, 1996, I made the best decision of my life; I made Jesus Lord and Savior of my life and was baptized.

With Jesus as my Lord, I learned to deal with my physical episodes differently and rather than becoming worried because I could not control them, I prayed. Prayer helped me cope and took away my worry, but it didn't take away the physical weakness. I went to get more help from doctors to figure out what was going on, but the answer was the same as before; they had no answers.

One evening in 2005, while sharing my struggle with one of my sisters in Christ, she alluded to the possibility of me experiencing some form of anxiety. She was familiar with anxiety because she suffered from obsessive-compulsive disorder. Ten years had passed since I first started battling these unpredictable episodes, and for the first time someone gave me a clue. After my friend left my house that evening, I consulted Google for answers and sure enough, after much research, I learned that I was experiencing panic attacks. I was dealing with post-traumatic stress disorder (PTSD), most likely triggered by my past traumatic issues. The only solution was therapy.

I was not happy with my diagnosis due to my dad's mental history, but I was tired of experiencing such unpredictable attacks. Although I was scared to embark on this journey, I quickly made an appointment with a counselor and he confirmed my research. This led to the long, painful journey of exposing my past and dealing with the scars it left. This journey taught me to forgive my parents and those who had hurt me, including myself, in a way I never had before.

Through much prayer, spiritual support and therapy, I am able to accept that I am broken, and God can still use me. Some dreams were stolen, but God has given me new ones. Because of my pain, I hurt others and myself intentionally and unintentionally, but with God I can find forgiveness and make amends with others whenever possible. In therapy I was reminded that in order to embrace who I am and become daily who I desire to be, a woman pleasing to God, I must never be afraid of looking into my past.

My days of weekly therapy turned into months, months turned into years and years turned into healing. After years of prayer, God made it clear that I was in need of intense therapy. He saved my soul on May 26, 1996 and 10 years later he opened my heart to experience healing from my past. He gave me a new beginning.

I am so grateful for the years of counseling I received. I was able to see clearly God as a Father who loves and protects me. I developed a deeper gratitude for Jesus' sacrifice. I built the deepest and most loyal friendships, including my husband. I learned to accept the things I could not change, including accepting my dad, for who he is, not who I want him to be. I learned that I don't always have to cry alone when I am hurting. I learned a lot of things, but the one that will stick with me from this experience is that we can hide from our pain, but it eventually finds us.

If it was up to me, I would run and hide from pain, but God has taught me that if I confront it, the blessings I receive are more than I could ask or imagine; it may even be a new beginning.

Olivia Hudson

2
Between a ROCK and a HARD Place!

It took me years to realize that one of the best places to be in life is between a rock and a hard place, because then, and only then, was I truly able to see God at work in my life. In the past, it was easy to fix my own problems when I saw several solutions that I could control and manipulate to achieve the end desired result. This is one of the primary reasons I believe the bible says in Matthew 19:24, *"It is easier for a camel to go through the eye of a needle than for a rich man to enter the Kingdom of God."* Why might you ask? Because the "rich man" believes he has all of the resources available to fix his own problems. He, in essence, with all his wealth, talents and possessions, becomes his own god.

Think about that for a moment. We are no different than the "rich man" God referenced. We may not have millions; however, we have food on the table, a place to lay our heads, a vehicle, a job (or a source of income, even if supplied by the government), talents, and yes, like the "rich man," some successes. Therefore, like those who are "rich," it can become very difficult for us to see our need for God, because sometimes, we can allow those blessings to become our gods.

In the book of Hebrews (12:11), the bible teaches us, *"No discipline seems pleasant at the time, but painful. Later on, however, it produces a harvest of righteousness and peace for those who have been trained by it."* Thank God for boot camp! I thank God for signing me up for early morning training, even when I didn't feel like attending. I have to trust that God knows the battles that lie ahead of me, and He knows the training (or the discipline) I need to prepare for those wars. I must trust His training program, and accept the obstacle courses He allowed in my life... for MY good.

Can you imagine your life without any discipline? Can you imagine how your children would be if everything they ever wanted were immediately given? More importantly, can you imagine how you would respond during a difficult trial (e.g. financial crisis, health crisis, etc.) if you never were trained through hardships? In other words, how could you possibly run on faith, and live in peace, during very difficult trials, when you were never trained or disciplined by any hardships? That's equivalent to running a marathon without any preparation whatsoever. Get the point?

I have a friend who lives a very *comfortable* lifestyle. She once confided in me, "I have never been in a situation where I saw God as my only option." That statement resonates with me to this day! At first, I was tempted to feel like God must love me less. Then, I immediately thought to myself, God loves me just as much, and I am grateful for the trials I have endured because then and only then was I truly able to gaze upon His majesty and see His deliverance.

One of my favorite passages to respond to that "trouble" is in Romans 4:18-21. It states, *"Against ALL hope, Abraham in hope believed... without weakening in his faith... he did not waver through unbelief regarding the promise of God... being fully persuaded that God had power to do what he had promised."* If you have ever been delivered from extremely difficult trials, that passage should give you chills!

When you are out of options, and your talents, your beauty, your intelligence, your career, your strength, your relationships, your possessions, nor your bank account can rescue you, and your only option is to look up and see God, and call on His name, praise God! Because not only will you see His deliverance, you will quickly discover that it was Him all along who was carrying you, and allowed you to have those possessions and attributes in the first place.

In case you are wondering, I speak from experience. I was abused as a little child, and witnessed my mother being physically abused on many occasions. In fact, one night, we both were attacked and had to run for our lives from the man in her life at that time. I was homeless at the ripe age of 11 or 12, along with my mother while fleeing from his abuse. We found ourselves in downtown Milwaukee, Wisconsin without a penny to our name. I grew up on welfare/government assistance most of my youth. One year, we moved over 20 times because either we didn't have the money to pay rent, or was fleeing from abuse.

I could go on and on and on describing my "boot camp," but what matters most is the outcome. Because God rescued me, and provided for me during those times, I learned how to be disciplined, how to persevere, and most importantly, how to expect the impossible when ALL odds were against me.

As a result of God's glory, I became a Christian as a teenager. As a result of God's glory, I was blessed to graduate from college. Ironically, it was the same college down the street from the bus station where

I once stood a few years prior (Marquette University). I am still growing, learning, and looking to God for His constant guidance in my life so that I can be of help to others in need.

I thank God for knowing the right times to corner me between a rock and a hard place because I need His constant reminder that He exists, that He cares, and that to this day, He delivers me from all my troubles. Psalm 50:15 say to *"Call upon me in the day of trouble; I will deliver you."* I have learned from years of being rescued that being *"refined by the fire"* (1Peter 1:7) is a good thing, because of what it produces in me. For this reason, I thank God for His preparations and training in my life. I can't imagine where I would be if I never experienced seeing Him as my only option.

Zenja Glass
www.UnlockingGreatness.com

3
A New Stage of Life

There I was in the company of friends, enjoying my friend's bridal shower. I was having so much fun, until a friend I was just getting to know made a statement that made the rest of my time seem to past really slow. You would think that someone said something mean to me, or something that hurt my feelings but that wasn't the case, the statement she made entered me into a new stage of life.

My passion for helping women, led me to developing a friendship with a young sister in Christ in her twenties who had only been married for a few months. We began to have weekly talks. By God's grace I was able to impart some wisdom from my twenty-two years of marriage to my friend who was in her twenties. She asked if my husband and I could mentor her and new her husband and we gladly said yes.

My friend lived about an hour and half away from her mom, and although her mom wished she could have gotten together more often with her, she was unable to do so. When her mom, found out that I was spending a lot of time with her daughter, providing guidance and support, <u>she was very grateful</u>. I can relate to her feelings because no matter how old my children are, if someone takes good care of my "babies", that person wins my heart. That's exactly what happened, I won the heart of her mom, even though we had only connected in person once.

During the bridal shower, we talked like we were old friends and she again expressed the gratitude she felt for me loving her daughter. As we talked, my young friend walked into the party. When her mom saw her, she greeted her by saying; "Hi, look it's your two moms." She must have felt my energy change because she quickly changed it to, "I mean your mom and your spiritual mom." I laughed at her statement but inside I was like: you think I am like a mom to your daughter.

Later that night, I told my husband what happened, he responded with, "Hmm. Interesting." His brief feedback made me dig deeper into that comment. So a few days later, I shared with someone, who is older and wiser than me, about this strange interaction. "Well Olivia, seems like you are shocked" she said. "So let me ask you, how do you view yourself in the relationship?" "Like a friend helping a friend," I replied, "Not like a mom helping a daughter." She then pointed out that my friend is only a couple years older than my oldest son. In shock I replied, "Oh my gosh! I really could be her mom. I AM an older woman."

I was hit with the lemon of: it's time to accept you are over 40 years old. My wise friend reassured me with, "No worries, you are young at heart. This information is good so that now you can tell how young women may view you." I was no longer a young gal, but an older lady.

I decided to study what it meant to be, "an older woman". I studied Titus 2:1-5, focusing on the role of older women. It was different since I always looked at it from the younger woman's perspective. There was an expectation for older women in Titus. The scriptures made it clear that my role is to set an example and train the younger women in the things I should be practicing everyday. Things that will not lead anyone to malign the Word of God.

After learning about my role as an older woman, I asked three young married Christian women whom I had known for a few months if they were open to allowing me to teach them what I'd learned over the past 22 years of being a disciple, a mother, a wife, a friend, a daughter and more. I shared that I still had a long way to go but I wanted to live out Titus 2 and it would be an honor if they allowed me to practice with them. They responded unanimously, "We will love it!"

Becoming aware of the fact that I have entered the older woman club was very humbling. God rescued me from an empty way of life (1 Peter 1:18) and allowed me the privilege to teach younger woman how to be women pleasing to God. I am in awe of how God has transformed my life and wrote a different life story for me, so I am going to savor this new stage in my life.

I still have a lot to learn as an older woman. I'd like to conclude with the words from a book, "I Love Growing Older, But I'll Never Grow Old." by Kalas J. Ellsworth: *"Even at its best our life on this earth is one where, as Robert Browning put it - our reach must exceed our grasp, "or what's a heaven for." We're almost certain to leave this life with some task unfinished, some dreams unfulfilled, some regrets still flying about the soul like a fly on a sweaty day. At times of such realization we should ask God's help to climb up Mount Nebo, and give thanks. Whatever this life has been, by God's grace and mercy, the best is yet to come."*

Olivia Hudson

4
911 - What Is The Nature Of Your Emergency?

I have only called 911 twice in my life: Once in the early hours of the morning for my Dad who was having trouble breathing and once when we found a possum in our bathroom at 2 a.m. Don't even ask about the possum---that's another story. However, each time I called, it was my last option---not my first thought. I usually respond to situations with a level head. I've been known to "white knuckle" many situations.

In 2000, I found myself calling out to God who is my emergency hotline. "What is the nature of your emergency?" was the reply. I said, "Father, I don't want to be here. I don't want to go through this. Please! This is not my issue." God's reply, "OK, I'll help. I'll send an ambulance, but be prepared, this is going to hurt."

Let me catch you up on the details about how I came to <u>need</u> to dial "911 God." My husband had gone to a meeting for Bible talk leaders at our church. During the meeting, they announced plans for a new program, "CR" (or Chemical Recovery group) that would take place in Boston, Massachusetts. We were currently living in New London, Connecticut (which was two hours away from Boston).

After the meeting, my husband found himself motivated to participate. He was ready to deal with the issues that had led him to abuse alcohol in his past. He asked me to join him for the meeting in Boston. I agreed to go - after all, it was so good that he was getting in touch with the demons of his past. Since I was the queen of denial, I didn't go to the meeting with a heart ready to learn or to be moved. I went because my husband asked me to come.

When I arrived at the meeting, I immediately wanted to leave. I could not believe that I was facing a room full of people who hurt others, a room full of alcoholics. This was so hard and it brought up so much pain for me, but I was not willing to deal with any of my pain. As I sat there, I thought about the fact that both my dad and husband are alcoholics.

The people at the meeting talked about the pain they had caused others just like my dad and husband had to others and me. It was hard to sit through the whole meeting, but I pushed on and I knew I was critical and very unsupportive of my husband. But I didn't know how to handle the pain. I did not learn how to handle the pain until later after working on myself. So, sadly I did what I knew best: I became self-centered and withdrew.

Despite my actions, my husband consistently attended the recovery group. I will always be grateful for the friend who attended every session with him and helped him along. In the CR group, participants were asked to write a journal listing each use of alcohol and/or drugs and the consequences. I can still remember the deep sorrow my husband felt as he got in touch with the destruction and causalities of his choices.

Just as my husband had needed a friend to attend the meetings with him, another person later needed me in the same way. A Sister-in-Christ needed a partner to attend meetings with her and to be her support along the way. Two other sisters had tried to attend with her, but it was too hard for them. I took on the challenge and I am so thankful that I did. God had me exactly where I needed to be. Watching my sister work through her pain allowed my heart of resentment and un-forgiveness towards my husband and father to soften.

I learned to show compassion to these people as I watched them hurt and feel such despair and powerlessness over their addictive natures. Before attending the meetings, I had no compassion for them.

Every time a journal was read, I cried because it was so obvious these addicts were hurting. There was so much hurt in that room.

Over time my heart became softer and, eventually, God gave me the courage, and the bravery, to talk to my husband about the hurt and pain that I had felt as a consequence of his addiction. It was truly a miracle that, over time, our conversations about the pain led us to forgive each other.

God sent that ambulance (The CR Group) and it did hurt, but we are now healed. Both of us! Today I enjoy an incredible marriage because of the healing we experienced during that time.

After my husband graduated from the program, both he and I went on to lead the recovery group for our home church. I am grateful to say that many friends have also enjoyed this gift of healing.

Dona Casey

5
A Moment to Remember

My dad suffers from severe mental disorder, which means I've never had a consistent dad and, sadly, the dad I wanted and needed was never available. All my life I longed to connect with him, to talk with him, get advice from him, and not be scared of him. What I really longed for was a miracle. In January 2014, God blessed the desires of my heart, perhaps only for four days but it was the best four days in my relationship with my dad. God allowed him to have a moment of lucidity where I got to have what I desired most: a connection with my dad.

I flew to Panamá after hearing the news that my dad was not doing well; he hadn't eaten in a couple of weeks. My uncle's exact words were, "your dad looks like a living dead man; he doesn't look good". Everyone was concerned and everyone believed if something was not done quickly he was going to die. My siblings, my mom and I began to discuss how to help him. We all live in the US and he resides in Panamá because he was not ready to relocate.

As we talked, I realized something - my dad could die and in spite of all the harm he has done and all the people he has hurt, I love my dad and that was the only thing I wanted to tell him, not over the phone but in person. I wanted my dad to know how much I love him, forgive him and accept him, and that I will always care for him. I wanted him to know that I have taught my children to accept and love him not as the grandpa they would like but as the grandpa they have. I needed to share my heart with my dad and I was compelled to do it in person. My feelings were so strong that I picked the next available day I could fly. Once I talked to my husband I flew to Panamá shortly after getting the news of his health condition. My brother graciously agreed to take time off of work so I would not have to go by myself.

When we arrived, my uncle met us at the airport and drove us to my dad (he still lives alone, although he shouldn't). When I saw him my heart dropped; the man I knew growing up was no longer there. He was weak, could barely walk, and had no smile. Instead he cried, but he was happy to see us. He was shocked that we traveled to see him but he said he had a slight suspicion that something was happening. We found somewhere to sit and talk and I told him how much I loved him.

As I talked, tears flowed from my eyes and he tried to comfort me by saying, "don't cry. I am OK." I quickly dried my tears and said, "dad you are not OK. Look at you and this place. What's going on?" He took the opportunity to share with me what was on his heart. "I have done so much wrong in my life and I have hurt so many people. I was not a good father or husband. I was not nice to people. I have daughters and I never got to walk any of them down the aisle to give them to their husbands. I believe that God is using me as an example of what happens when you do so much evil."

I was so moved by the way he shared, with such sorrow, that I felt great compassion for him and longed to bring him relief from the pain he was feeling. I knew I didn't have the power to heal my dad from such pain and that only God could do such a thing. I told my dad that maybe God wants to have a different story with him, a story where he shows the world what it is like when a sinner repents.

To my comment he replied; "Olivia I have done too many bad things." I asked if he were sorry and he said yes. I said I forgive him but it was up to him to find a way to forgive himself. For the first time in my life, I had the courage to tell my dad that I believe he had never accepted his mental illness. "You are probably right." He replied.

Talking to my dad like this was amazing. I must confess that after years of praying to talk to my dad in the way we were talking and not seeing it happen began to rob me of my faith that such a prayer would ever be fulfilled. However, in spite of the level of unbelief I had developed I somehow managed to hold to a mustard seed of faith and occasionally prayed that God would allow a miracle. And God did!

I was there to witness my dad as he apologized and confessed all the sorrow he felt for the harm he had done, all the regrets he had for thinking more about himself instead of what was best for his family. It was a miracle and how awesome it was that God chose me to be there. I must be a very special person.

The rest of my time there was amazing. We read the Bible together, we prayed and he came to church with me. We went to see his doctor, visited family, and went shopping for clothes for him to wear to church. He had lost so much weight that his clothes didn't fit. I took him out to a nice restaurant to eat after church and we talked and talked for hours.

The night before I left, my dad asked me if I was dying. He said that something was different about me - the way I talked to him, the way I talked about God. It was a faith building moment to say to him that I was not dying and that I came to say I love him and I am who I am today because of studying the Bible and learning God's way. I opened the Bible and shared many scriptures with him on the love of God. He said "Olivia you know I know what I have to do is hard and I am scared because there is a lot to change." We ended our talk and went to bed. My cup was overflowing with gratefulness for the time we got to spend together. The next day as we traveled to the airport I could tell he was sad. I was sad too; I honestly didn't want that moment to end.

Sadly my dad's moments of lucidity are gone and he is back to his paranoia and multiple personalities; in fact, I am getting ready to go see him because he is not being responsible about taking his medication and is creating a lot of problems. I also hope to plead with him to go see his mental health doctor on a consistent basis.

The truth is, as I write this I am grieving because I may never have that moment where my dad and I spoke just like I imagined in my dreams. But there is another truth and this is the one I will hold on to when I am sad: God is good to me. He gave me a desire of my heart and for four days I connected with my dad. For four days I savored the dad my heart desired and that is a memory I will hold in my heart forever.

My dad is deteriorating and I don't know if he has months or years to live. Every time I get a call about him, I take a deep breath for I know one day I will hear that he is gone. My prayer is that when he dies it will be with him praising God. But no matter how he goes, I will always love him and remember him not as the one who caused pain to others, and me but as the one who brought healing to my heart on January 2014 in a hotel room in Panamá City, Panamá.

Olivia Hudson

6
Unexpected Blessings

My second son, Miles Winston Grossett, was due to be born right before Thanksgiving. It was the best thing that had happened to our family of three. Floyd, Riley (his seven-year old big brother) and I had cried, prayed and waited for several years as we suffered through four miscarriages before Miles.

I remember being pregnant with the baby who would become Miles and wondering if he too would be another child that I would never meet. I felt robbed as a mother. I had four babies I never knew. I would never touch their toes or brush my cheek against theirs. The pain of their stolen lives was agonizing. It was hard to believe that it could actually happen on this fifth try – that a baby would grow inside of me once again and be born.

I read an article about how mothers who have miscarried have a hard time giving their heart to new children because they feel that they are betraying the ones that were not born. That was me. I felt guilty about being pregnant again and about everything going so well. I was afraid that my children who had died would be forgotten.

The turning point in my pregnancy with Miles came when it occurred to me that if those other children were alive today, they would be thrilled that I was pregnant with their little brother or sister. They would be so excited as they looked forward to a new baby in our home! At that moment I was able to completely give my heart to Miles, and believe that we would actually meet him.

During that time of grief and confusion, I learned to view life from God's point of view. I realized that to God, every life has value no matter how long that life lasts. Life is to be celebrated, whether someone lives for one day in the womb or 100 days on earth – or even 100 years. I resolved to be thankful for any other children God would give me, no matter how long they lived, whether I got to meet them or not.

Miles was born almost two weeks late on the first day of December. We were crazy about him! Miles had arrived - we could hold him in our arms and smother him with our kisses. I wish I could say that we lived happily ever after without the threat of more children dying. But when he was just nine days old, Miles was lying unconscious on an operating table while a surgeon performed a procedure that ultimately saved his life.

Needless to say, after all that we had been through for Miles to be born, our resolve was tested in an unbelievable way when we learned that he was born with a life-threatening birth defect. How we made it through this scary time is the story I want to tell.

One day shortly after he was born, Miles stopped eating in the middle of the night. I tried to nurse him unsuccessfully for several hours until almost noon the next day. And he was so sleepy – I couldn't keep him awake. Then came the projectile vomiting and I called the doctor. That telephone call set into motion a chain of events that I will never forget.

In less than two hours, Miles and I were in the pediatrician's office. I explained that he was not nursing and that I was having a hard time keeping him awake. Then with a sober look on his face - and to my surprise - our pediatrician urged me to take Miles to the newborn intensive care unit (NICU) at our local hospital immediately. He told me Miles was "very sick" and that he did not know whether the problem was with his nervous system or digestive system.

At the NICU, Miles was taken out of my arms and his little, newborn body was strapped onto a hospital bed. Wires were everywhere, wrapping around him and connecting him to noisy machines. I was still clinging to the idea of an easy fix. Was it the broccoli that I had eaten the day before that might be the problem? I held his blanket and waited for Floyd.

After several hours, the NICU specialist asked for our consent to take Miles by ambulance to Yale Medical Center an hour away. There were tests that could be performed at Yale to properly diagnose Miles that were not available at our local hospital. My heart was torn when we learned that we could not ride in the ambulance with him, so we followed the ambulance with an empty car seat.

At Yale, we met the surgeon on call. Her staff prepared Miles for testing with unruffled urgency. They spoke kind words of assurance to us as we strained to understand the new vocabulary used to describe what they were going to be doing with our son. Soon the answer came: Miles' intestines were twisted and blocked due to a birth defect, and he needed surgery. He had not been able to keep food down because it had nowhere to go. By ten o'clock that night, about twelve hours after my initial telephone call to his pediatrician, Miles was getting prepped for surgery to correct the problem.

Floyd and I called Riley, and Riley asked me one of the hardest questions I have had to answer as a mother. "Is my brother going to die?" What could I say? The surgeon had been positive and assured us Miles would be fine. But we had already lost four of Riley's brothers or sisters whom we had never met. Miles was the baby who was not supposed to get sick and die. While we waited, Floyd and I surrendered ourselves to the idea of losing Miles. And I remembered my decision before Miles was born to celebrate a life no matter how long it lasts. I told Riley: "Everything is going to be okay, you'll see."

Just like in a movie, the surgeon came out of the operating room when she was done and the world stood still. We listened, as if in a dream, to her explain how Miles' intestines were only slightly twisted and there had been minimal damage since we had caught his condition in time. We heard her say that the surgery was successful, and relief washed over us. Miles was no longer in danger.

As Miles recovered in the hospital there were ups and downs. At one point, when everyone expected him to make progress, he seemed to be going backwards. It was heartbreaking to imagine more needles and more invasive procedures being done to his little body if he did not recover quickly enough. During this time, I asked the question I could no longer hold back: "God, why? Why was Miles born with intestines that didn't work? I've already lost four other children - why this test?"

I remembered Jesus' interaction with a man who was born blind from birth. Here was someone who had a birth defect like my son. Jesus' disciples asked him who had sinned – the man or his parents. I could understand the jumble of feelings behind their question. It is so easy to want to assign blame in a situation like this – to blame ourselves and even blame God. Jesus said, *"Neither this man nor his parents sinned, but this happened so that the work of God might be displayed in him"* (John 9:3)

After meditating on Jesus' words, I surrendered to this one rule of spiritual life: that some things happen or do not happen so that God's work and power are obvious in our lives. What begins as a curse unexpectedly becomes a blessing. Four children whom I have never met have become a blessing to me as I look forward to seeing them in heaven. If a birth defect could display God's work in Miles' life then I knew that none of this would be in vain if we could continue to trust in a God who is always working – sometimes invisibly - for the good.

Today Miles is a healthy five-year old

boy. He is playful, daring and smart. He has no idea how fragile his life once was. But maybe that is the point. We are all at the mercy of God's timing, and yet in spite of that we must live without hesitation, move courageously forward through hard times, and wait patiently for God to display his greatness in each of our lives.

Tamara Grossett

7
A Cinderella Story

As a little girl, I dreamed of having a dream wedding; but sadly, I made choices that did not produce what my heart desired. My husband and I were married... on his lunch break. Crazy, I know. After three years of marriage we asked God to be the one to guide us and His love and grace has allowed us to enjoy years of love, loyalty and faithfulness to each other.

One day, I told my husband that I wanted to save money to celebrate when we reached twenty years of marriage. He happily agreed. Years passed and we were now months away from celebrating twenty years of marriage. We had saved enough money to have a Cinderella reception.

It was so much fun to plan such occasion. Eventually everything was done. The facility and the catering service were picked, our guest list was complete, and we made arrangements to pick up our guest from the airport. Our coordinator, Annie Fields, was amazing! She made it so hubby and I did not have to worry about anything and just enjoy this time.

As we planned the agenda for the evening of the party, we decided to surprise our guest by doing a special dance. A dance that would represent how we felt about our marriage. After going through the elimination process we picked, "Time of my life" from the movie Dirty Dancing, It was perfect; we have been having the time of our lives for the past twenty years!

We came up with our own choreography and after practicing for some time showed it to a dance instructor to get her professional opinion and advice. With tears in her eyes, she said, "your dance is perfect, it tells a story and it is so clear that you are in love." She gave us a few tips on facing our audience and allowed us to use her studio for rehearsals. Wow! We left her studio feeling so encouraged and ready to show it to our friends.

As time passed, our excitement grew, and the party could not come fast enough. But every Cinderella has to have a story and I have mine. Six weeks before the big event my husband called me and said, "Honey, I injured my foot playing ball, I don't know how bad is it but I am on my way to the ER." My heart sank; I knew this meant no dance.

He ruptured his Achilles and immediate surgery was required. Instead of feeling sorry for my husband, I was upset with him, as if he injured himself on purpose. My husband took notice of my face of disappointment and said, "Honey, I am so sorry, but don't worry, I WILL dance with you."

His surgery led to some complications and he ended up having three more surgeries due to infections. My husband was so weak; the last time I had seen him like that was ten years before when he had meningitis. As I cared for him my heart changed, I just wanted him to be better. I prayed, God I am sorry I had been so focused on the anniversary party and the dance we were supposed to do that I forgot the reason for the celebration, which is no matter we never let anything stop us from being one, as you desired.

Yes, this was important to me, but not more important than my husband so I decided to let it go and pray he will be well enough so we won't need to cancel our party; but even if we did, I was surrendered. I felt more in love with my hubby after my heart got in the right place. I loved how he actually believed that he would dance with me.

Three weeks before the party he was well enough to walk in crutches, so the party was still on! However what my hubby did next really reminded me why I love this man so much. He said to me; "we can do the dance, I can get a one-legged orthopedic scooter and we can practice, we have three weeks. We can do it. We already have the steps we just need to make some adjustments since I only have one working leg." I was hesitant but I figured we had nothing to lose. We got the scooter and got to work. We had so much fun practicing that even if it didn't work out, we were building great memories, so it was worth it.

I was amazed at how well we were doing, so after a couple of weeks of daily practice we went back to the dance instructor for feedback. This time she became very emotional and said, "guys it is beautiful."

The big day came, my husband looked so handsome in his Navy dress white chokers and I wore a beautiful gown. I really felt like Cinderella. Everything was beautiful, Annie turned the ballroom into a magical room with her decorations. As everyone enjoyed the party, my husband and I snuck out of the ballroom to change. He changed into a silky lime green shirt and black slacks and I into the most expensive dress I have ever paid for: a soft silky dress that flowed gracefully with every move I made.

My husband entered the ballroom and stood in front of our guest and began to tell the story of how we met, and how we got to where we are. He ended the story with this statement, "...and I have been having the time of my life ever since." A soon as he ended retelling our love story, our son Joe took away the crutches and handed my husband the scooter, which we kept hidden during the whole party. The song began to play as I walked in and I could feel all eyes were on me: I was having my Cinderella moment. Although all eyes were on me, I saw none except the man I have loved for twenty years. I was ready to dance.

As I was walking I could hear the sound of surprise in everyone's voice. It is funny how I didn't care, all I could think about is how much God loves me. As we danced, I felt like I was floating, I felt more in love with my husband at that moment.

Since the injury prevented him from lifting me in the air like Patrick Swayze lifted Jennifer Grey, we made adjustments. I climbed on the front of the scooter and he'd spin the scooter with one hand, held my back with another hand and I leaned back and opened my arms open to the heavens. It was an epic moment.

The dance instructor had given me some advice that made all of the difference: I needed to trust that Cory had me, that he would not drop me and to lean as far back as I could. Every time we practiced, I was scared to do it, but on the night of the celebration, there was no fear at all. I trusted in my husband because he had me for twenty years so far and never dropped me. So I leaned back as far as I could and enjoyed that moment! I felt like Kate Winslet when Leonardo DiCarprio asked her, "Do you trust me?" in the movie Titanic.

I'd finally got my Cinderella party and dance. This memory reminds me of Psalm 37:4, *"Take delight in the Lord, and he will give you the desires of your heart."* No matter how big or small the dream.

Olivia Hudson

Wow

Truly a Cinderella Story

8
The Promise

I had been married for two years. We were having the normal arguments couples have, yet were still committed to each other and to God. But then, something happened that allowed me the opportunity to draw closer to the promise that God would work everything out for my good.

One day, we were planning the final details for a two-week vacation. We were looking forward to it and we needed it! The doctor called and gave us the unexpected news that my husband had cancer. Although the news was hard, we spoke to the doctor and he said it was OK to go on vacation and then deal with it when we returned. It was our desire to do so. I am so glad we got the OK! We had a good time and added priceless memories to our marriage. We returned from vacation knowing what lay ahead. Somehow I had been able to enjoy our vacation without being consumed by the news of his cancer.

Once we were home, I had to face reality. My husband had cancer and we had only been married for a couple of years. Hurting inside, I knew that this would affect all the plans we had made for the future.

We started chemotherapy and it immediately affected his health. My husband was placed on a waiting list to receive a donation for a new liver. He had always been a very active and independent man and had never been sick a single day since we married. Now, not only was he sick, he was very dependent on me. He was in so much pain and it was hard to watch him be so weak.

As I write this, we are still in the process of dealing with his cancer, but I am learning so much already. I am learning that all the things about which we would argue, fuss or fight were so insignificant. I wish I could go back to those times when I allowed myself to become upset with him to the point I would go lay on the couch. Now, all I want to do is lay next to him and place my head on his chest, but I can't because of the pain that it causes on his sore body.

I cannot remember the last time I was able to sleep for two straight hours before being awakened by the agony of his voice telling me that he is hurting and the pain medications are not working. I feel so helpless because there is absolutely nothing I can do to help him.

In the midst of trying to be strong for my man, we received a letter from the health insurance stating that they will only pay out a certain amount of coverage. Thus, financially, this is hard because his short-term disability has not taken effect yet.

I wish that this were all I had happening in my life so I could focus only on my husband, but that isn't the case. We have two German Shepherds that require attention. I am trying to be a support to my daughter and her two beautiful daughters as she is trying to make a better life for herself and my granddaughters. I am also trying to enjoy my newly married son with my new daughter-in-law, guide my younger son as he gets ready to graduate from high school, and encourage my second daughter as she tries to figure out what direction to take her life.

This time in my life is very challenging. I have learned very quickly that there is only so much I can do. I have had to learn to rely on my faith. I trust that God will continue to strengthen me with his love, grace and mercy. In the midst of this storm, its clear to me that God has taken care of me. I can say without hesitation that I have been able to do far more than I could have imagined, not by my own power but by His power.

I choose daily to focus on the promise that God works for the good. Focusing on John 16:33 allows me to face that in this world we will have troubles, but focusing on

Jesus helps me to overcome the troubles I face in this world. That focus allows me to find victory in the midst of my storms.

"And we know that in all things, God works for the good of those who love him, who have been called according to his purpose." (Romans 8:28)

Irma Bryan

9
Out of My Comfort Zone

"What do you want to be when you grow up?" This is a question adults ask children. "A veterinarian," I would scream, because I loved catching little critters down by the creek and I loved biology. Ministry was never a consideration.

My father was an officer in the military so I grew up moving about every two years. I was born in Germany and lived there two additional times and spent my junior and senior years at a military base high school in Taegu, Korea. Moving around had several benefits: It was fun and amazing to see the world, and experience different cultures. When I lived in Korea, we would travel to places like Japan to play other sports teams. Family vacations were taken to the Philippines. I learned to make friends quickly and adapt to new environments.

The downside is that it was hard to develop deep lasting relationships because they were always changing. It became more about making new friends than keeping old, because chances are I would never see the old relationships again. This also extended to my family. My nuclear family was close, but I didn't have much time with grandparents, aunts, uncles, or cousins.

Also, while I have always been good at making friends initially, my personality is more introverted and quiet. I struggle with people pleasing and trying to be who I think people want me to be rather than just being myself. I remember moving to Korea from Virginia in my junior year and deciding that I would not choose a style of music I liked so that I could fit in with all groups of people. Even in Korea, the music you listened to defined the group you associated with.

I became a Christian when I returned to the states and moved to North Carolina to attend the University of NC at Charlotte. Although I went to church every Sunday, I knew that something spiritual was missing in my life. It was God and making Him my Lord and Savior. One of the toughest areas for me to repent of was in being honest with others and learning to love people. I remember being asked to pray for an endearing personality.

During my college years I dated and married an amazing brother in our campus ministry, Gary Sciascia. He loved God and me. He was very discerning and had a heart for God. He became a teen minister while we were still dating and in college. Ministry has been his dream since that time and we both did ministry full time in Atlanta, Georgia and then again when we moved to Connecticut.

I love being a disciple of Christ, however it was never my dream to do ministry as an occupation. Many things that the ministry requires are things that I'm not good at naturally, such as connecting with others. My husband and I currently lead a fairly large church and presently we work with campus students. Although I love working with campus girls and teaching them to love God at such a young age, I've had many days wondering why God chose me for this. My husband is so strong at ministry things and I'm so weak. The ministry requires skill sets that seem to be my weaknesses.

I've shared publicly about my weakness and somehow it encourages people. I wish I could say, "And now thanks to God I'm great at connecting with others". Not so. I'm growing but it's still a challenge. I pray often to have a bigger heart for people and to see what my blocks are to loving them and giving my heart to them fully. When I see sisters who are strong at connecting with others, I have tended to feel jealous and insecure, but now I'm learning that I can learn from their strengths instead. Interestingly enough, as I've been open about my struggles, more women have talked with me about their struggles to connect with others.

One of the bible characters I connect most with is Moses. When God calls him, it is not at the height of his youth and strength, but when he is old. And he doesn't feel adequate to lead. He's the opposite of Isaiah. Isaiah said, "Send me". Moses said, "Send someone else". God does not try to build Moses up but tells him it's not about him (Moses) but about Him (God). This is always the message God tells me. It's not about you, but about Me.

But Moses said to God, *"Who am I that I should go to Pharaoh and bring the Israelites out of Egypt?"* And God said, *"I will be with you. And this will be the sign to you that it is I who have sent you: When you have brought the people out of Egypt, you will worship God on this mountain."* (Exodus. 3:11-12)

God is turning my lemon of inadequacy into lemonade of growth in my dependency on Him. I've been a Christian for 26 years and if you are not careful, with the passage of time you can stop growing. There is plenty of room to develop my relationships with others. I need not fear these areas of weakness. I am excited and look forward to changing.

Gail Sciascia

10
The Great Comforter

Three years had passed since the adoption of my daughter. And yet, as honored as I had felt about God having given me the privilege to adopt, I grieved. I grieved that I never had the chance to buy special items for my own "little baby girl." My dream of becoming a Mom to a baby girl included the experience of buying things for her to wear as she came home from the hospital.

I had been able to buy dresses for my daughter - lots of pink dresses - since the day she arrived at the age of two and loved it! Still, every time I shopped for a friend who was having a baby, or whenever I saw a newborn baby girl, it triggered in me a bit of sadness because I never had the opportunity to shop for my baby girl.

One day, as I grieved, a gentle voice inside me whispered, "Don't cry. You can still go shopping." What happened next is a memory I will forever treasure.

The voice continued to say, "Shop for Jasmine as if you were buying stuff to bring her home as a baby." In my mind, I thought, "No way, that is crazy. People will think I am crazy too." But then the voice said, "Silly you. It's not like you have to announce to the store what you are doing." To which I thought, "Great point." So I put on my shoes, told my family I was going out to run errands, and went straight to Wal-Mart.

This shopping trip became a great time of healing. There was such rush of emotions! I felt like I had lost my mind, but I also felt so happy to be experiencing what I was doing. I walked around the baby aisle and picked out a cute baby blanket with polka dots, a lavender bottle with animal designs, a cute monkey rattle, some pink bootees, a little pink outfit, a girl bib that said "Everybody loves me," a pink newborn hat, and a pair of pink hand mittens. I must have walked around for an hour just savoring this section.

When I finished shopping, my heart felt a sense of peace with not having carried a baby girl in my tummy. I can't explain it. But, all of the sadness I had felt for quite some time was no longer there.

As I drove home, the voice again whispered to me: "Remember how you though of Jasmine as a baby girl when you brought the baby gear. The baby girl in her needs to be loved. Share with her your trip."

When I arrived at home, I found a basket into which I placed and arranged, very nicely, all of the baby gear I had bought. I walked into Jasmine's room, sat on her bed and said to her, "Jas, I want to show you something. I know I didn't give birth to you or see you as a baby, but if I had, these are the things I would have bought for you."

My daughter's response made me grateful to God. In spite of how stupid this shopping trip may have looked or sounded to others, even myself, God knew it was needed to bring healing to me and joy to my daughter. With tears in her eyes, my eight-year old daughter said: "Thank you so much Mom. I can't believe you went to the store and brought this for me! That you thought of me as a baby as you were shopping. I wonder if my biological mother did this, but it doesn't matter because you did this for me." And she gave me a long, huge hug. I comforted her as she cried over her loss.

Together we enjoyed every item in the basket. She was in awe! When we were done, she asked if she could keep the basket, to which I said, "No. Mommy is going to keep it." As I left her room, the voice again whispered: "It's time to let go" It was not My plan for you to carry a daughter.

I sat on my bed on cried, it was a

quiet cry, and no one heard me. As I was crying the voice again whispered to me very gently: "It is not My plan for you to grieve over what you did not get. It was always My plan that Jasmine would be your daughter. I knew she would need you. I put the desire in your heart for a girl because I knew Jasmine would need a mother who desired to have a Christ-like mother-daughter relationship. That is exactly what Jasmine needs in order to have a chance to do great things in My name. It's time to let go and stop grieving over what you did not get."

I am convinced that this voice that spoke to me, although it may have sounded like my conscience, was the voice of God. For only God can think of a way to heal and nurture two hearts in such an unexpected way. I know it wasn't me; I don't have that kind of power.

That day I made a decision to let go and to never again feel sadness in my heart about not having carried a baby girl in my tummy. Next, I went back to Jasmine's room and told my precious girl that she could keep the basket. I did, after all, buy the things for her.

Three years later, the basket is still sitting in my daughter's room. She says that if she has a daughter one day, she will dress her with the stuff in the basket. The pink blanket has become one of her most treasured possessions. It warms my heart to see her sitting on the couch with the pink blanket on her legs.

Weeks after doing this with my daughter, I was having a conversation with a dear friend as Mother's Day was approaching. We were sitting in her car and she cried as she vulnerably shared with me what she goes through every Mother's Day. Her mother died when she was two years old. Although she loves being encouraged on Mother's Day by her two girls, that day makes her feel sad because she never got to know her mother.

She never got to talk with her or get advice about raising girls. She grieved the memories that never happened. This special day in the calendar created to bring joy to many, had brought sadness to many who had either lost their mother or never met her. However next Mother's Day will be different for my friend because after hearing my friend's pain over the loss of her mother, God led me to encourage her soul.

God, in his amazing love for his people, placed it on my heart to go out to shop for my friend on behalf of her deceased mother. My friend had shared with me what she knew about her mom. This led me to assume that her mom had been an incredible woman.

I went to the store and purchased a book. I wish I remembered the title, but I know the book was something about a mother's love. I also brought her a card that said "how proud I am of you my daughter." Inside I wrote: "I believe with all my heart that your mom would have told you the words on this card, because you are an amazing woman." I also bought chocolate, tissue, a journal and a few more knick-knacks. I placed all the items in a basket and gave her the basket on Mother's Day. I asked her to open it when she knew she could dedicate an hour of solitude to it. She agreed. I was anxious to see what she thought.

Two weeks later she opened the basket. I will never forget how impacted she was. She said it brought her much joy. She was able for the first time to not focus on the loss of her mom but on the fact that she made her Momma proud. She was so grateful. I felt such an honor that God used me, an imperfect woman, to show such amazing love.

I can echo the words of Paul in 2 Corinthians 1: 3-4: *"Praise be to the God and Father of our Lord Jesus Christ, the Father of compassion and the God of all comfort, who comforts us in all our troubles, so that we can comfort those in any trouble with the comfort we ourselves have received from God."*

God brought me comfort. And from that comfort, He led me to comfort my daughter and my dear friend.

I will forever be reminded of what happens when I listen to His voice!

Olivia Hudson

11
Finding Freedom in Forgiveness

Since the days of my childhood, I had heard all kind of stories about "karma:" the idea that things will "go bad" in your life if you do something wrong to others. When I was 19 years old, I did something terrible. A very close friend of mine became pregnant. She was very confused, scared, and she had no support from the guy or her family. Another friend suggested an abortion as a way to "solve the problem." After much talk, it was decided she would terminate the pregnancy.

The day for her appointment came and I went with my friend, standing next to her through the whole process. I remember not sleeping for days after. I wondered what she was thinking, but was too afraid to ask about it.

Sometime later, I could not take the guilt anymore. I decided to confess this deed to someone I greatly respected. After hearing me, the person told me that I participated in a horrible action. Not only had I never taken the time to sit down with my friend to ask her feelings, but also I had never spoken up about my own beliefs with her. I had not stood up for the moral choice nor had I offered to support and protect her in her time of vulnerability. I was told at that moment "God will never forgive you. And if something ever goes wrong with you, just remember what you did that day."

Years passed and I enjoyed a successful career and a quiet life. However, I always wanted more and more to add to my professional life. I had many dreams and goals, but getting married was not one of them. Even though marriage was not part of my plan, I met a guy, fell in love, got married, and had a baby. It all happened very fast.

Three months into our marriage, things started "going bad." At the very beginning, it was not that bad, just simple "cultural disagreements" - as he called it most of the time. I became pregnant with our first child and our disagreements became worse day by day. My husband is in the military and, sadly, I started noticing that each deployment or underway was peaceful for me and for him. I realized we needed extra help and tried to look for marriage counselors. Sadly, we both were stubborn and not ready to change. Having never lost contact with my friend who had the abortion, I talked to her about the problems with my husband. Unhappy herself, my friend opened up about her life and having been told that she would never be blessed with children. I told her I believed I was being punished for what we did when we were younger.

Although there were a lot of problems in my marriage, we managed to conceive a second child. I sought professional help for our issues and my counselor told me I was experiencing "emotional abuse." It was the first time I had heard of such a thing. She asked me why I was staying in this kind of relationship. I never answered her, although I knew the response. This was my punishment. I deserved this because of karma.

There were many things that went wrong in our marriage. It was not only my husband, but also me. I became a master of not talking after a fight. I could go for days or weeks and it was not helping the relationship at all. There was a night in which we had a big fight and he did not come home to sleep. I remember laying face down on the floor asking God, "Why?" I had so many questions: "Why did you let this happen? Why did you let us get married in first place? I know I did something horrible, but how much is enough?" I cried for so many hours, so loudly, for the first time. Before I had always cried in silence in the bathroom or I would bite on a pillow so that the children would not hear me. I asked God to take my love away for my husband and to give me the courage to divorce him. I told God that if He was not going to let me leave my husband to show me why I should stay.

Three years later I was invited by a dear friend of mine to a women's Bible group that, in turn, led me to begin personal Bible studies with one of the ladies of the South Sound Church of Christ. I started learning how God is love and is filled with compassion. I realized that he is not a God of revenge and that he is not in the business of punishing us forever. I had never talked about what I had done at the age of 19 with anyone else since my confession, but I decided to open up to the ladies in my Bible study. We talked about how I had felt since the day I sat by my friend's side as she terminated her pregnancy.

I felt less heavy in my heart when I learned that God had never left me alone. The suffering I was experiencing was not the product of God's punishment or a result of karma. My choices to live by my own will had led to my unhappiness. I talked to my friend about how God is love and merciful. I asked her forgiveness again and we cried for about an hour together. It was a healing time for the both of us.

The more I read the Bible, the more I fell in love with the scriptures. I also fell in love with my husband again and I learned to forgive him for any pain he had caused me. I asked for forgiveness for any pain I had caused him. Eventually my husband started studying the Bible and now we are learning how to make God the center of our lives and marriage.

It's amazing to see the changes in our lives - to watch and enjoy the man my husband is becoming. I am grateful God gave me the courage to stay and fight for my marriage. I witness daily His miracle. He showed me people can change, and that having Him as the center of your house, can create the most amazing home.

12
God Always Has A Plan

As I think about my life as a Navy wife, moving is something that comes along with the package. There are times when you have a say in where you live and other times when you don't. These are the times that I know God is truly in control. This became very obvious to me early on when we got orders to Charleston, SC. When I was initially told about Charleston, I was not happy about these orders.

Why couldn't we move back to the Northeast closer to family which was much more familiar and comfortable to me? My quiet and stern heart response was, "There is no way I'm moving to Charleston." What about my support group, which was my church family? And on top of that, I had just found out that I was pregnant. I felt like I needed to go some place where I would have the physical and spiritual support that I had had during my other moves.

Although my heart was unsettled, I remained quiet on the outside. But inside, my stubbornness persisted. As my grumbling left my heart, I remembered Daniel 5:5, *"Suddenly the finger of a human hand appeared and wrote on the plaster of the wall, near the lampstand in the royal palace."*

I knew the "handwriting was on the wall," and we were off to Charleston. The move came shortly after hurricane Hugo hit. I can remember how, as we came closer to Charleston, the trees on the side of the highway looked like someone had taken a buzz saw and cut them all in half. My heart sank as I wondered how in the world I was going to live in a place like this with my husband heading off to sea.

After our arrival in Charleston, we sat down that evening and watched the news. There in front of our eyes was my husband's newly assigned ship with the headline that it had just left the day before for a six-month deployment to the Persian Gulf.

We sat there in shock because this meant that my husband would be leaving in a few days for training in Virginia and then immediately fly off to meet the ship in the Middle East. This would leave me all alone to adjust to living in a new city with a one year old and to being a few weeks pregnant. This posed a very challenging decision for me to make, "Should I stay and settle our young family in Charleston or should I move to New York and stay with my family until my husband returns from sea?"

I decided to stay in Charleston. After that decision was made, my husband had just a few days to move us into an apartment and off he went to his deployment. My first priority in Charleston was to find doctors for my daughter and myself. This appeared to be a very simple task. My daughter was able to see a doctor at the Naval Hospital which would naturally mean that I would more than likely be able to see an OB/GYN doctor there also. My daughter's first appointment went very well, so I proceeded to the family practice clinic to make an appointment for myself.

Inquiring about an appointment for myself, I informed the receptionist about my pregnancy. Then everything appeared to grow dark as she waved a piece of paper in front of me. Her words appeared to be jumbled together. Reaching for the paper, she repeated herself again saying, "I'm sorry, ma'am. We are not accepting any new OB patients. Here is a list of doctors. You will have to find one yourself."

I could not believe her words. Didn't she know whom she was talking to? Didn't she want to know about all the troubles I had with my last pregnancy? Didn't she care or even want to hear why I needed to be seen there? I felt rejected and alone. My husband was gone and I had no one who could help me find an obstetrician. With the paper in my hand, I slowly walked away thinking how difficult and scary this was for me because I had previously lost a baby and had had a challenging pregnancy with my daughter.

Still, I began my quest. With my list in hand, I sat down and I started dialing the numbers on the paper, beginning with the first one and working my way down the list. Call after call, I was met with the same words: "Sorry we are not accepting any new patients right now." I began to feel more and more alone and discouraged and finally whispered, "God, I really need for you to help me because I don't know what to do."

When I made the next call, a very pleasant woman answered. She said she could make an appointment for me in a few weeks. I was so excited! God had heard and answered my prayer. I thought I had found the doctor I needed to see! Yet, after I answered her question, "When did you find out you were pregnant?" alarm filled her voice. She then informed me that their office would not be able to see me because I needed a very specific test done within the next few days. Her voice sounded more disappointed than I felt. She urged me to find a doctor that could see me this week in order for the test to be done.

Believe it or not, this was the best news I had received during my many telephone calls, because now I had a mission! I knew that it was God answering my prayer. This was the one certain criteria for which I needed to look - a doctor who could see me in a few days. And I knew that doctor would be the one God had picked out for me!

After a few more calls, I reached an office that could see me within two days. I was so excited! It appeared as though God had parted the Red Sea for me to cross! A couple of days later, I arrived at the doctor's office and was greeted and welcomed by a friendly staff. A tall man named Dr. Robinson warmly introduced himself to me. We hit it off immediately. During that visit I found out he was a fellow New Yorker (which always creates a bond) and that he was familiar with some of the places I knew well. I was able to get my test completed and felt that I was in good hands.

I must tell you that when women say, "Every pregnancy is different," it is so true. All of my appointments went well. My only challenge was eating; I only ate because I needed to, nothing tasted well. Every appointment would end with us sharing a story about New York. Time seemed to fly by quickly and before I knew it, I was about four weeks from delivery.

Walter's ship was due back on August 16th and the baby was due September 11th. That would be plenty of time to get adjusted and ready for the new addition to our family. But a couple of weeks before Walter's return, I woke up with terrible pain and I thought, "Please, baby, only a few more weeks." At the following checkup appointment, everything turned out to be fine.

The day before my husband's arrival I was so excited I couldn't wait for us to be a family again in less than 24 hours. My daughter and I would have her Daddy home! I don't know if you can imagine the excitement that is in the air when family comes home after a long deployment. Seeing family members and children laughing, hugging and crying tears of joy was everywhere you looked! It was a wonderful day filled with excitement! Our family was whole again! Little did we know that our family would grow again---the very next day!

I woke up early the next morning excited to see my husband lying next to me, but a little sad because he had to return to work and stay overnight. Still, I was grateful that he was home. I quietly got out of bed and went inside the bathroom. I was met with a wave of pain. I wasn't sure what to do. I thought this couldn't be labor because the baby wasn't due for another three and a half weeks. I quietly sat at the end of the bed.

When my husband saw me there, he

asked what was wrong and I told him I think I'm in labor. He hopped out of the bed and off to the hospital we went. My husband had only been in Charleston for a few days when we first moved there and had no idea where the hospital was located. So I had to give him the directions to take us there. We arrived at the hospital at about 7:15 a.m. By the time Dr. Robinson arrived, our baby was ready to enter into the world. In between contractions, an introduction of my husband and my doctor was made. By 8:33 a.m., our son was born!

Although it was quite shocking and unexpected for the baby to arrive early, I was grateful that everything worked out. In just two days, our family had grown by two. God had come through again, not just with the doctor that I needed for the prenatal care and delivery, but also with my having my husband by my side and a healthy baby boy!!!

Melody Channell

13
The Peace Box

During my childhood keeping the house clean was not an option. My dad will get us up two hours prior to school to clean the house. As an adult I followed my parents passion to keep a clean and presentable house. However, when I became a mom, keeping the house clean and teaching my children to keep a clean room (which was all they were required to clean without my help) was no easy task.

I wasn't too demanding in keeping the house clean, I only wanted thing to be placed where they belong! It's not complicated to pick up a sock in the middle of the room instead of walking right over it, or it is obvious dishes do not automatically become clean from sitting on dressers, also I think everyone knows that the chair is not a linen or coat closet. I found myself like a drill Sergeant, saying, "pick this up, pick up that up, put this away, put that away" every five minutes. Maybe not that close, but it felt like it to me.

It took me years to realize that I was

like a dripping faucet when it came to cleaning. By years I mean one of my sons had already left for college at the time of this realization. It was amazing how a small item on the living room couch or floor, that the kids didn't put away, will set me off.

I knew my problem wasn't the stuff laying around, it was I didn't feel appreciated by my kids, because I will clean while they were gone to school and they will come home and throw things around. I began to take personally their lack of care. I forgot they were children, not adults!

One morning while cleaning, I was getting frustrated again at all the stuff lying around the house out of place. As I picked stuff up in frustration a little voice came to me and said, "Girl, you know these are kids, you kept things super organized growing up because you were afraid to get severely punished for making a mess. Your kids feel safe with you so they will test you. Remember, constant bickering is not working. Try something else."

And just like that the Peace Box was born one afternoon in the Hudson household. I began to clean and as I found different things that belong to the kids I placed them in a box. I wrote on the front of the box the following text: This is the Peace Box, when mom find stuff while cleaning where they don't belong I will put in here. If this box gets full, the stuff inside will be dropped off at Goodwill.

When the kids came home I introduced the box to them and made them aware of the stipulation that was not written on the box; "Some of the things placed in there may get broken, smashed or claimed by others." Surprisingly, they loved the idea.

The Peace Box has never gotten over half full. One thing I love is that I see how my children care for each other. If one of them notices something belonging to their siblings inside, they go warn them that they should get it out – before they lose it - Forever! It didn't matter what it was: clothes, shoes, game systems – all gone forever.

Honestly, having the Peace Box reminds me of the scripture in 1 Corinthians 14:33a; *"For God is not a God of disorder but of peace..."*. It was born out of frustration (and it does NOT look cute in my living room); but I am so grateful that God showed me that it was pointless to keep nagging my kids about picking up their stuff. As a parent I will have bigger problems to deal with, so I figure the Peace Box can take care of the little ones!

Olivia Hudson

14
An Unexpected Journey

By nature I have always been a healthy, happy, active person who tries not to bother my mind with too many worries.

One day, my family doctor called me to say that it was time to do several routine health exams. I had not had any of these exams before because I did not have health insurance. But, since I had just turned sixty-five, I now qualified for Medicare. Also, I had promised to take care of my physical health by having an entire set of routine tests done once the insurance was available. Now, I was ready for the tests - thanks to my doctor's follow up. My doctor said I had been on her mind and she had checked my files to see why. I asked her, "What should we do first?" "A routine colonoscopy," she replied.

The colonoscopy preparation wasn't as bad as I had expected. Secretly, I had hoped I'd lose a few pounds! The procedure itself seemed uneventful. Once it was completed, I found it strange that others had already left the room while I was still there. The nurse brought my husband, Ken, into the room and said that a gastroenterologist would be right with me. "Wow." I thought, "How nice of the doctor to give me all this attention!"

After the doctor walked in the room, he said, "We found something that we biopsied and the results will be back tomorrow." I remember him saying, more than once, that what he found looked suspicious. Both my husband and I remained calm and positive. We decided to believe that it was probably nothing and waited until the next day, which turned out to pretty much be business as usual. I made calls to family and friends about my doctor visit and that evening I went off to church.

The next day, sitting in the doctor's office with my husband at my side, the doctor told me that I had rectal cancer. He tenderly explained that I would be seeing a surgeon and an oncologist, and that I would need more tests. I gasped for breath and then cried, "This can't be." I just kept saying over and over, "God help me, God help me..."

The doctor and my husband walked with me as I left the office. I didn't want anyone to see that I had been crying; however, as soon as Ken and I entered the elevator, I started crying again. I stopped as the door opened, because the people there were waiting to get on the elevator. I just didn't know how to handle this news. I wasn't expecting anything like this to happen to me. I was speechless.

The days moved slowly. There were so many family and friends with whom I wanted to talk. I asked everyone for prayers as I was girding up for the battle. I texted, e-mailed, and made calls trying to remember to contact everyone I knew who loved me.

I remember talking with my son and he said something that helped me during this journey. He said, "Mom, you can not afford yourself any negative thoughts." His words of wisdom led me to cling to this scripture: *"We demolish arguments and every pretension that sets itself up against the knowledge of God, and we take captive every thought to make it obedient to Christ."* (2 Corinthians 10:5) To make it through this illness without losing my mind, I had to take captive every thought.

During this time, I felt God carrying me the whole way. There were times when I didn't even feel like my feet were touching the ground. I constantly begged God to please help me to do this well (whatever that was supposed to look like since I had no clue). He provided. I had new best friends, my oncologist, and my surgeon. I felt so loved and cared for by God.

God even provided laughter right

before I went into surgery. My daughter brought all sorts of silly dog pictures on her phone that kept me laughing. My husband was my constant and loyal companion. He silently enjoyed our laughter.

The surgery went well. The doctor was able to remove all of the cancer! I felt like one lucky lady - considering that I had been preparing for the worse. Even the doctors were celebrating that it was not as bad as it had seemed. The news that everything was gone was so overwhelming I could hardly take it in! I am so thankful to God!

I had to have several follow up visits to confirm that all the cancer was gone. From now on, I will continue to need a colonoscopy every year, but I am okay with that. My body works a little differently since the surgery, but that, too, is OK.

As I reflect on this journey that I hadn't expected, I sometimes start to cry. I am so grateful for the lesson God taught me that if I trust in Him, even with the unexpected, I will come to understand on a deeper level the meaning of 1 Peter 1:7-8: *"These have come so that the proven genuineness of your faith—of greater worth than gold, which perishes even though refined by fire—may result in praise, glory and honor when Jesus Christ is revealed. Though you have not seen him, you love him; and even though you do not see him now, you believe in him and are filled with an inexpressible joy"*

My faith has been refined! And, because of this experience, I praise, glorify and honor God more today than before the day I found out I had cancer.

Dona Casey

15
Surprise Gift

God must know that I love surprises, because He always tends to surprise me with the most amazing gifts. On June 1, 2014, he gave me a beautiful gift that I will treasure forever. He allowed me to get a glimpse of what 1 Corinthians 2:9 says: *"No one's has ever seen or heard anything like this. Never so much as imagined anything quite like it - what God has arranged for those who love Him (MSG)."*

On May 29, 2014 I flew to Honduras, one of the most dangerous places in the world to live at this time. This was not my first visit. I had been there in January 2014, to serve with H.O.P.E. Worldwide Medical Brigade. I went with my son Joe, who was graduating from high school that year.

Every evening after a day of serving the poor, all the volunteers enjoyed a time of fellowship. During one of the evenings, I had the privilege to fellowship with Dulce Cruz (the Women's Ministry Leader of the San Pedro Sula (SPS) Church). I was very moved by her love for the women of SPS. As we got to know each other, I shared with her my journey to face the scars of my past and all the intense therapy I had undergone. After I shared my story with Dulce, she not only related to me but opened my eyes to truly seeing how privileged I was to have been able to afford to see a counselor to help me navigate such traumas. I love how God uses every opportunity to keep us grateful.

At the end of our talk, she mentioned that it would be so great if the sisters there, including her, could receive such help. She wished so much to do more for the sisters who may be stuck spiritually, weak, or in need of that extra encouragement to not give up on following God. She told me that my story was similar to many of the sisters in SPS. Sadly, their financial resources are limited. They can rarely afford to host disciples to come speak and teach classes. She added that sometimes people are afraid to come since it's so dangerous and she understands that hesitation.

After listening to her, I told Dulce that I would love to come with my husband and perhaps help in some way. I knew we were not experts, but we are always honored when God presents an opportunity for us to share how he has worked and continues to work in our lives. Dulce said she would love to have us come speak. Honestly, I thought she was joking! After I returned home from the brigade, I mentioned to my hubby that it would be awesome if we could go and do a marriage class; but he mentioned that it would be impossible for him to go due to his job. Being in the NAVY, it would be hard for him to receive approval for time off to travel to a country with a safety warning.

I was sad to hear that both of us going was not an option at the time, but the desire to help the church in SPS was very strong in my heart. I considered going by myself, but I didn't think I could help that much. This was my insecurity speaking.

One night I asked my husband, how would he feel if I went alone to SPS to teach a class on self-care to the women in the church. He replied, "It will be scary. But if God put it on your heart, you should go because we can't live by fear." So after praying, God helped me to see that there was a message I could share with the sisters in SPS: we don't have to live as unhappy Christians - we can get help. I learned that lesson on my journey to recovery and healing. I was open to sharing my journey and God using my pain to help others.

I called to Dulce to see if her invitation for me to come was still open. As soon as she said," yes," I then asked my husband for a plane ticket to Honduras as a

Mothers Day present. He was happy to purchase that gift for me!

On May 29, 2014, when I arrived at SPS, I was greeted at the airport by sisters who were so happy to see me back! We went to lunch and they gave me the agenda for the next four days. They were eager to get started.

Every day was filled with my teaching a class and then facilitating group discussions for either married, single, spiritually single and/or college sisters. I also facilitated a mother-daughter discussion group that was unifying for all involved. Every day was filled with deep, heartfelt conversations. Every night I was exhausted, but I went to bed eager to get up and do it all over again the very next day.

I enjoyed every minute of my time there! I became part of the SPS family and was treated like a sister by all - even the brothers! Hector, Dulce's husband, became very protective and urged me to be sure to get enough rest. I felt so loved and cared for by my new brothers and sisters.

I was so moved by the way God was using all the tools I had acquired through therapy. As an adult, I spent years in therapy seeking healing from growing up in a dysfunctional family. I was wounded by the emotional and physical abuse I experienced while growing up with a severe mentally ill father and a weary mother. It took time, effort, support and tears to finally arrive at a place where I am now at peace with the demons of my past. God enabled me to provide guidance that was biblical and practical for my Sisters in Christ in Central America. I did not deserve to have such an opportunity, but I am so grateful that God used me, an ordinary woman, to do great things for Him.

To conclude my time there, the sisters of SPS had asked me to preach. Prior to my arrival in Honduras, the sisters wanted to schedule a time where they could invite their friends to come and hear me speak. I gladly accepted their invitation to preach.

On that Sunday morning, I woke up and had a great time of reflection with God. I was truly in awe of all He had done through me during the past three days. I was nervous about preaching, but ready to be used by God.

When I arrived at the church, everyone was so excited to hear me speak! The sisters were eager for me to meet their friends. Some gave me handmade gifts, cards and souvenirs. One sister in particular told me that although she had no money, she wanted to give me something to remember her as a thank you for the time I had spent with her. She gave me one of her favorite necklaces. I was so moved that words cannot describe how impacted I was. The fellowship was overflowing! The service hadn't even started and I had already lost count of how many women with whom I had connected through talking, taking a picture or receiving a gift. The fellowship was rich in every way.

    The moment came for me to preach. I was so nervous as I walked up to the beautifully decorated podium. However something miraculous happened as I faced at least 300 women - unexpected by me but planned by God - who stared at me with eager hearts. The fear was gone! Once I saw that so many women had come to the service, I was convinced that God had a message he wanted me to share with the sisters in San Pedro Sula and their friends. The message wasn't, "we don't have to live as unhappy Christians." The message was *"With God all things are possible"* (Luke 18:27). That is the message He taught me and continues to teach me everyday.

    God gave me an unforgettable surprise when he took the pain and sorrow that controlled my life for many years and showed me what I could do with it all if I stay close to Him. I can now inspire others to do the same.

Olivia Hudson

16
Grass Does Not Grow Under My Feet

I've been told many times that grass does not grow under my feet and that I can do circles around people! My mom used to joke that she needed to make an appointment with me just to talk. (By the way, she lives with me ☺.) My weeks were filled with bible studies, getting together for breakfast or lunch with other sisters, building relationships with women I had met, and meeting the needs of my husband of 23years, and our family. Life was busy and it wasn't perfect.

I still had the issues and problems that many people face. For example, our oldest daughter decided to leave God during her teen years. After 2 years, she rekindled her relationship with God and is now doing well. Our youngest daughter became pregnant as a teen. That was a wild ride to say the least, but I love Nana's "cutie petutie" - my grandchild. I have two sisters who have been diagnosed as bipolar and are in need of my continued support.

My mother also needs some care. So needless to say, life has kept me on my toes. But throughout all that has happened, and although my faith was shaken, I have held on to God even if it was only by a thread. I know that is where some of us are right now. Life has been moving on some days a step forward and 2 steps backwards, or vice versa.

Then, the last weekend in April of 2014, my life took a radical turn. I woke up extremely fatigued on a Sunday morning. I had had a busy week beforehand with family in town for Easter and my grandson's first birthday. I figured I overdid it. My body crashed and rest was needed. By Wednesday, I was experiencing weakness in my left arm. I couldn't process information clearly. I had a slowed speech pattern. The left side of my face felt like it wanted to droop and/or become numb. And, I was still extremely fatigued. After getting CT scans of my brain, a brain and cervical spine MRI, and a spinal tap---which was torturous, I was diagnosed with Multiple Sclerosis (MS) in July.

To say that emotions were high is an understatement. Although I believed that God had a purpose for me, guilt, sadness, frustration, a sense of worthlessness and other emotions clouded my view of all the blessings God had given me. I realized I had to surrender my heart, change my mindset and know, without a doubt, that God was in control and had a purpose. Next, I allowed this incurable disease to be an opportunity, not an obstacle, to glorify God. With this resolve in place, I have seen my character challenged and realized what is important: to love Him and to be obedient. MS has strengthened my relationship with God. As I travel through these unchartered waters, I have seen God's love through my family and friends. They have prayed with and for us, prepared meals, made phone calls and sent text messages for which I am so grateful and by which I am humbled.

    It's been six months since the onset of my symptoms as I write this. I wake up every day not knowing how my day will proceed because my symptoms vary from day to day. Between the pain, fatigue, and weakness - which are the major culprits right now, I know that I must hold on to the scriptures that give me hope, comfort, and peace. I don't know where this disease is taking me but what I do know is: *"Though the fig tree does not bud and there is no grapes on the vines, though the olive crop fails and the fields produce no food, though there are no sheep in the pen and no cattle in the stalls, yet I will rejoice in the Lord, I will be joyful in God my Savior."* (Habakkuk 3:17-18)

So, although I do now have grass under my feet and no longer do circles around people, yet I will rejoice in the Lord, my God, and be joyful in God, my Savior.

Carmen Spearman

17
My Milagros

Since I was a teenager I made a decision to have two children, a boy and a girl (obviously I had no clue that it was not up to me!). I always wanted a daughter and that is a desire I believed God placed on my heart because He knew it would lead me to fulfill His will to unite me with Jasmine; it would lead me to my Forever Daughter.

Although God has blessed my husband and I with four boys whom I love very much, my husband and I decided to adopt a baby girl. Before embarking on that journey we sought advice and one of the pieces of information we received was to do foster care to see if we could handle five children. So after many house inspections and lessons, we became licensed foster parents.

Shortly after our certification, we provided care for one child for seven months. After the child was returned to his parents, we felt ready to adopt so we went through the process of becoming certified adoptive parents. While waiting for our certification to change, we received a call during the Christmas Season that a two-year-old little girl needed a foster family. Although we had decided to not do foster care anymore, it felt wrong to say no to a homeless child during the holidays so we said yes to her. Unknown to me but known to God, I had just accepted my Forever Daughter.

The first time I saw Jasmine was in the Safe Home (a temporary home for kids removed from their families). I visited her there for four days before I brought her home. The day I took her home to live with our family, she cried so much. She didn't want to leave the Safe Home. The Safe Home staff and kids had become her family in just ten days. It was so hard to see her suffer. Hearing her cry pierced my heart and I tried to comfort her by talking, but it only helped a little, so I took her shopping.

We went to Pier 1 Import, which was the closest place and she picked a comfy pink pillow that she used to sleep at night for weeks. Once we arrived home, the boys were very welcoming and Jasmine was not afraid to blend right in with the family. It was like she had been part of our family her whole life.

Three weeks later the sweet little girl we had welcomed into our home developed serious behavior problems. It was like we were at war with a two year old.

She became disrespectful to any authority in her life. She seemed to find pleasure in contradicting me. There were times I really didn't like her at all and could not wait for her to be reunified with her birth mother. I was trying so hard to help her feel loved, but it seemed like everything I did made her angry. The fact that she would one day return to her biological mom allowed me to persevere and train her in spite of her outbursts.

Time passed and since reunification to her biological mother was taking longer than expected, I prayed to God for wisdom on how to help Jasmine and help me to not lose my mind at the same time. It was clear I needed professional intervention, so I decided to go to therapy to learn how to help Jasmine. I continued to pray daily that her mom would change so they could be reunited. Aside from Jasmine's behavior problems, I sincerely didn't want her to have to deal with the pain of losing her biological mother.

In therapy I learned that everything that was going on in her life made her fearful and insecure; instead of her becoming like a sweet puppy that will cuddle with you when they are afraid, she became like a porcupine, painful to get close to. My counselor helped me see that if I truly wanted to help Jasmine, I needed to fight for her to be her best.

Jasmine needed help knowing that she no longer needed to control her life and that God placed us in her life to take care of her. I was seeing Jasmine as a victim of her circumstances, therefore, I was not having expectations for her and that was creating chaos between us.

I saw that in order to stop viewing her as a victim, I needed to pray daily to love her as if she were my own child and not be afraid to give myself to her or set boundaries for her. This decision was like trying to clean up the leaves that fall in my backyard; just as it seemed I made progress the wind blows and the leaves are all over the place again. I felt discouraged on a daily basis.

After a year of having Jasmine, the social worker called and said that she was going to be put up for adoption and she wanted to know if Cory and I were willing to adopt her. WHAT??? I thought to myself this is not supposed to happen. I am supposed to just be her FOSTER mom; this can't be part of God's plan. Was I not praying faithfully?

I shared the message with my husband as soon as he arrived home from work and after listening he said, "if she doesn't go back to her biological mom then she stays with us. We are her family now". Inside I was like, WHAT??? How do you not even take some time to think before you say something like that? How did that decision come so easy to you? Why didn't I feel the same way? What if her behavior never changed? Can I handle such constant rebellion daily in our home? Can I put up with the daily screaming and the battles in public? What is wrong with me? Why can't I just say yes? Jasmine is an innocent child and I am an adult. I felt so ashamed of my feelings and I really didn't want to say yes, but I was afraid to say it out loud. I was afraid of being judged. This was not the adoption story I wanted.

My heart was troubled and although no one could see it, I am so grateful that God could and He knew exactly what I needed. I know I needed to pray but I didn't want God to remind me of James 1:27, *"Here are the kinds of beliefs that God our Father accepts as pure and without fault. When widows and children who have no parents are in trouble, take care of them."* As I wrestled with all my emotions, I realized that my struggle wasn't just whether or not we should adopt Jasmine. My real struggle was could I love her like I love my sons whom I birthed.

Before I lost my mind processing all of this, I took a drive to see my sister in Christ Kim and to spill my heart to her. I knew God could hear me but I needed someone to help me to hear Him. Kim allowed me to speak and sob until everything in my heart was out. After l was done she gently asked me, "Olivia, what if you found out you were pregnant by surprise? Would you keep the baby or abort it?" Without hesitation I said I would keep it. She then said, "What would you do if you found out before that child was born that it had special needs? Wouldn't it be like most babies and will require extra care?" Again without hesitation I said I would keep my baby. She looked me in the eyes and said, "Jasmine is your surprise baby and she has some special needs."

At that very moment I heard the voice of God clearly announce to me "You are pregnant". I was pregnant with a 4 year old that was wounded, and He chose me to be the mother who would care for those wounds. God allowed me to hear that Jas needed a mommy and all the things that most mommies would do for the child they bore - love them more than they love themselves. I will always be grateful that Kim was led by the Holy Spirit to speak the truth to me in love (Ephesians 4:15).

Another profound thing Kim shared with me that morning was that the first step to falling in love with Jasmine and loving her as I do my sons is to accept that this is the will of God. She said, "some gifts have to grow on us; we can't beat ourselves if we don't like them right away and we first have to decide to accept the gift and then to appreciate it and believe it is exactly what we need, especially if it's a gift from The Lord." By the time I left Kim's house, I was at peace and ready to be a mommy!

After much paperwork November 29, 2009 arrived. My husband, our sons, mother-in-law and a few friends sat in front of the judge that would legalize our decision to welcome our daughter. During the ceremony, Jasmine whispered in my ear every two minutes "Am I a Hudson now?" After what seemed like forever I said "You are now a Hudson," and she grinned. Jasmine became my daughter. I had my girl!!! When we left the courthouse, she was excited to announce her new identity! God gave me a daughter and what an amazing girl God picked for me. Through her pain, she has loved me. Because of her, I have learned more about what it means to stay committed in a relationship during the hard times and to love even when the feelings aren't there.

At the time I write this, my daughter is 11 years old and she is a very kind and loving girl who is learning how to deal with her hurts in a healthy way. My daughter loves me and I love her and our love for each other has allowed our relationship to blossom and to weather the storms that take place in our relationship. I don't know what the future looks like or the things we will have to work through as she grows into a young woman, but I believe God picked me to be her mom because I can teach her to learn to trust God even when she is hurting, as I have, and continue to learn that lesson in my life. I can teach her to fight to accept no less for herself than what God wants for her and ultimately to not listen to Satan's lies, no matter how loud he speaks.

God handpicked Jasmine for me. He wrapped her beautifully and he continues to give me wisdom in caring for this very special gift. I am not a perfect mom and she is not a perfect daughter but I finally believe that we are perfect for each other, for with each other we learn how to be more like Jesus. As long as I can remember I always wanted a daughter and her name was going to be Milagros. I have a daughter. Her name is Jasmine Milagros Hudson and she is my Milagros (Miracle).

Olivia Hudson

18
Jasmine's Story

One day as I was putting stuff away I found a short essay my eleven year old daughter wrote for her English class, I was so moved that when she came home I asked her if I could publish her story in my book, she gladly said yes. She was very happy that I wanted to put her story in my book; she didn't expect this at all and neither did I. I hope you enjoy reading it as much as I did!

A slice of Life

When I was two and living in Groton Connecticut, my hometown, I was with a foster family and they were my foster family then because my bio mom had made some poor choices. I used to think it was my fault but my foster parents always said "it's not your fault your bio mother made those choices" and that always hit (inspired) me.

As I got older I also started to understand that my bio mother didn't mean to hurt my bio brothers or me. I also started to understand that she made her choices and I don't need to suffer for her. That was the hardest part because I had to admit to myself that what she did and the people she hurt wasn't any of my concern.

Now that I am older I am more comfortable to tell people about my bio mom. I do talk to people about her mostly to express my feelings. I love my bio mother but she has hurt me intensely and I am still having a hard time forgiving her.

When I think of my bio mother I think about the sound of kisses smooch. I think of the second most beautiful lady in the whole in entire universe and knowing my Bio mother is as if tasting a piece of the most sour candy in the world. I say this because she did choices that hurt others such as herself and my bio brothers and I. The first most beautiful person in my life is my adoptive mother.

I was inspired to write this essay by Mrs. Middlebrooks my English arts teacher. It helped a lot to write this essay so all my thanks goes to Mrs. Middlebrooks.

Jasmine Hudson

19
Authors Note

Recently one friend recently email me the following letter:

Hola Amiga:
I am so sorry it has taken me this long to send you this. At this point I don't think you can use it --- too late. However, since I finally revisited it & finished putting my thoughts in writing I figured I can still share it with you. Thanks for inspiring so many of us to think back about those moments in our lives when God turned lemon into lemonade. There are so many different times in my life that He did just that! Here is one time - see attached.
Love ya
Abrazos y Besos,
Dami

I could not use her story because I was done with the editing and context of the book, however her email inspired the next story of the book.

This will be your story my dear friend, I will like to encourage you to make yourself a glass of lemonade and reflect on your life and write Your Lemonade Story because your story is worth writing!

To God be the Glory!
fantasticfivemama@gmail.com

Before you begin to write I will encourage you to reflect on Psalm 116 (MSG)

*I love God because he listened to me,
listened as I begged for mercy.
He listened so intently as I laid out my case before him.
Death stared me in the face, hell was hard on my heels.
Up against it, I didn't know which way to turn; then I called out to God for help:
"Please, God!" I cried out. "Save my life!"
God is gracious—it is he who makes things right, our most compassionate God.
God takes the side of the helpless;
when I was at the end of my rope, he saved me.*

*I said to myself, "Relax and rest.
God has showered you with blessings.
Soul, you've been rescued from death;
Eye, you've been rescued from tears;
And you, Foot, were kept from stumbling."*

*I'm striding in the presence of God, alive in the land of the living! I stayed faithful, though bedeviled, and despite a ton of bad luck,
Despite giving up on the human race, saying, "They're all liars and cheats."*

What can I give back to God for the blessings he's poured out on me?

I'll lift high the cup of salvation—a toast to God!
I'll pray in the name of God; I'll complete what I promised God I'd do, and I'll do it together with his people.
When they arrive at the gates of death, God welcomes those who love him.
Oh, God, here I am, your servant, your faithful servant: set me free for your service!
I'm ready to offer the thanksgiving sacrifice and pray in the name of God.
I'll complete what I promised God I'd do, and I'll do it in company with his people,
In the place of worship, in God's house, in Jerusalem, God's city.
Hallelujah!

20
Your Lemonade Story

Made in the USA
Middletown, DE
10 May 2015